Original title:
Holding on to Us

Copyright © 2024 Swan Charm
All rights reserved.

Author: Olivia Orav
ISBN HARDBACK: 978-9916-89-889-5
ISBN PAPERBACK: 978-9916-89-890-1
ISBN EBOOK: 978-9916-89-891-8

In the Hearts of Sacred Kin

In the dawn of grace, we gather here,
With whispers of love, and hearts sincere.
In unity we stand, hand in hand,
Guided by faith, in this holy land.

O light divine, our spirits rise,
In the sacred bond, where truth lies.
Through trials faced, we hold the light,
For together we walk, through day and night.

In every prayer, a promise made,
To nurture the flame, never to fade.
Bound by the ties of kinship strong,
In the choir of souls, we all belong.

With hearts uplifted, we sing aloud,
In the presence of grace, we are proud.
For in love's embrace, we find our way,
Together we rise, come what may.

As seasons change, our faith renews,
In the tapestry woven, we find hues.
With each shared joy, and every tear,
In the hearts of kin, God draws near.

The Covenant of Hearts

In the stillness where we kneel,
Our hearts entwined, a sacred seal.
With whispers soft, our spirits bind,
In love's embrace, the purest kind.

Through trials faced, our strength will grow,
Guided by faith, our light will show.
In every tear, a promise made,
A covenant in love, we've laid.

Sacred Echoes of Affection

In the chambers of our souls,
Echoes rise, as love consoles.
Each heartbeat sings a hymn divine,
In sacred trust, our fates align.

Through sacred space, our spirits soar,
In every glance, we seek for more.
With gentle grace, and hands embraced,
In love's sweet song, we find our place.

Prayers Invisible Yet Felt

In silent prayers, we close our eyes,
With whispers low, to reach the skies.
In faith we trust, though sight be thin,
Our spirits meld, where love begins.

Each moment shared, a blessing flows,
In every laugh, the spirit glows.
Invisible threads that bind us tight,
In love's embrace, we find the light.

Love's Unbreakable Covenant

In the shadows of the night,
Love's unbreakable bond shines bright.
Through storms we face, hand in hand,
In His grace, together we stand.

With every vow, our hearts ignite,
In unity's peace, we find our light.
As stars above in heaven's dome,
In love's strong arms, we find our home.

Beneath the Canopy of Divine Love

Under the sky, where blessings flow,
Hearts entwined in a gentle glow.
We gather here, in faith we stand,
Bound together by a Holy hand.

Voices rise, a sweet refrain,
All our struggles washed like rain.
In this embrace, we find our peace,
From all burdens, we seek release.

In silent whispers, prayers ascend,
To the Divine, where love can mend.
With every heartbeat, grace unfolds,
In the warmth of love, our story's told.

A Chorus of Souls in Harmony

In the stillness, a chorus we sing,
Together we rise, the joy we bring.
With every note, the spirit soars,
Echoes of love that forever endures.

From different paths, yet one in heart,
In this sacred space, we will not part.
Voices blend, a divine embrace,
Guiding us all to a holy place.

As stars align in the silent night,
We dance in hope, bathed in light.
In unity, we lift our song,
To Him above, where we belong.

Sacred Dance of Trust and Hope

In the rhythm of life, we find our way,
With trust and hope, we greet the day.
Each step in faith, a promise made,
Through trials faced, we are not afraid.

With hearts alight, we move as one,
Guided by love, our journey begun.
In grace we glide, through shadows and light,
Sacred dance, in the holy night.

With every twirl, we weave our dreams,
In the arms of peace, life's beauty gleams.
Together we rise, as spirits unite,
In this dance of love, our souls take flight.

The Song of Us in Silent Prayer

In stillness deep, our spirits meet,
In silent prayer, we find our seat.
A tapestry of souls entwined,
In the quiet, we seek, we find.

Voices hushed, yet hearts ablaze,
In sacred moments, we offer praise.
With every breath, we touch the sky,
Together in heart, as time passes by.

In this space, love's light will shine,
With humble hearts, we intertwine.
In the grace of silence, we clearly see,
The song of us, in harmony.

Bonds Forged in Divine Grace

In the quiet moments we seek,
A whisper of love in the breeze.
Grace wraps around hearts so meek,
Mending the spirit with ease.

With hands uplifted in prayer,
We find strength we did not know.
In unity, our burdens share,
God's light guides us where we go.

In sacred spaces, we gather,
Echoes of ancient hymns sung.
Hearts entwined, no more to shatter,
Our praises to the heavens flung.

Through trials faced and storms that rage,
Faith shines brightly in darkest night.
Together we turn the page,
In His presence, we find our light.

Each moment a blessing bestowed,
A tapestry of souls that weave.
In love's embrace, we walk the road,
In Divine Grace, we both believe.

The Light That Connects Us

In the dawn's tender embrace,
A glow stretches wide and far.
Across the universe's face,
We see love's singular star.

Threads of light bound us together,
Invisible yet strong and bright.
Through stormy seas or fair weather,
We rise as one in His sight.

Voices sing in harmony,
A chorus to the heavens high.
Together in this symphony,
We lift our spirits to the sky.

Hands clasped tight in reverence,
We walk the path of truth and grace.
In every heart, a residence,
Where kindness leaves its gentle trace.

Let us shine with pure intention,
Reflecting light in every place.
In our bond, a sweet ascension,
Love's glow a holy embrace.

Spiritually Entwined in Reverence

In the stillness of the night,
We gather 'round with hearts aglow.
With reverence, we seek the light,
In sacred space, our spirits grow.

Lessons learned from ages past,
Wisdom shared in softest tones.
In faith, our roots are held steadfast,
Together, we are never alone.

Each prayer a thread in the loom,
Weaving strands of hope and grace.
Through joy and sorrow, we consume,
A tapestry that time can't erase.

Bound by love that never wanes,
United by the things we share.
In grace, we rise above the pains,
With gratitude, in every prayer.

As we walk this path divine,
In reverence, our spirits soar.
In every heart, a sacred sign,
Forever entwined, forevermore.

Celestial Ties Across Time

Beneath the heavens, side by side,
We trace the stars with gentle hands.
In every heart, our spirits bide,
Connected in these timeless strands.

From age to age, our voices blend,
In songs of praise that fill the air.
Together, we will never end,
In every moment, love laid bare.

Across the epochs, our souls roam,
Bound by the light that knows no end.
In sacred spaces we find home,
In every stranger, we must befriend.

Each heartbeat sings of deeper ties,
In unity, we find our way.
Through trials faced, we rise and rise,
In faith and love, we choose to stay.

So let our spirits intertwine,
In every act of love and grace.
Together, through the years we shine,
Celestial ties, our warm embrace.

Anchored Hearts in Holy Waters

In quiet embrace, our hearts unite,
Cradled by grace, we find the light.
With each gentle wave, our spirits call,
Anchored in love, we shall not fall.

Through trials faced, we stand as one,
Guided by faith, our journey's begun.
In sacred waters, our hopes ascend,
Together we rise, on Him we depend.

The whispers of prayer, they fill the air,
Each murmur of hope, a divine care.
In troubled times, we seek His shore,
Found in His arms, we're evermore.

Beneath the stars, our trust shall flow,
In holy tides, our love will grow.
With anchored hearts, we lift our soul,
In unity blessed, we make them whole.

Our Souls' Unity in Faith's Warmth

In circles of light, our spirits blend,
With voices raised, our praises send.
Bound by the warmth, of love divine,
In faith's embrace, our souls align.

Through storms that rage, we stand our ground,
In shared belief, our strength is found.
With every prayer, the heavens part,
Together we heal, one faithful heart.

In quiet moments, we gather close,
In sacred bonds, we cherish most.
Each whisper of hope, a promise made,
In faith's warm glow, we are not afraid.

With hands entwined, our journey's clear,
In love's embrace, we know no fear.
Our souls united, a guiding flame,
In faith's warm light, we rise the same.

Celestial Tapestry of Togetherness

In woven threads of sacred grace,
We find our strength, we find our place.
Each color bright, each shade so sweet,
In tapestry's weave, our lives complete.

With every stitch, a story told,
Of love and faith; of hearts so bold.
In shared beliefs, we craft a dream,
Together we shine, a radiant beam.

As stars align in the night's embrace,
Our spirits dance, in holy space.
In unity's glow, we boldly stand,
A celestial bond, forever hand in hand.

Through trials faced and joys we see,
In this grand design, our hearts fly free.
With gratitude deep, we hold each thread,
In this tapestry, love's light is spread.

Kindred Spirits Beneath Heaven's Gaze

Under the sky, we walk as kin,
In every heartbeat, faith's light begins.
With every step, in grace we flow,
Kindred spirits, in Him we grow.

Beneath the heavens, our dreams take flight,
In unity's bond, we shine so bright.
With whispered prayers, our hopes ignite,
Together we journey, guided by light.

In moments shared, our laughter rings,
As joy abounds, our spirit sings.
In love's embrace, we find our way,
Beneath Heaven's gaze, we shall not stray.

Through valleys deep and mountains high,
In kindred hearts, we learn to fly.
For every trial unfolds a new grace,
Together we walk, in His embrace.

In the Light of Love's Sanctuary

In the calm of dawn, we rise,
Seeking wisdom from the skies.
Hearts entwined in gentle prayer,
Finding peace, our spirits bare.

In the warmth of sacred light,
Guided by love's pure insight.
Each moment shared, a holy thread,
Binding all, where angels tread.

Through trials faced and burdens borne,
A beacon shines in love reformed.
In unity, our voices blend,
As faith and hope we shall defend.

Let the light of grace surround,
In this refuge, love is found.
Together strong, we stand as one,
Beneath the wide and shining sun.

In love's sanctuary, we belong,
Hearts uplifted, singing strong.
May our spirits rise above,
In the light of endless love.

The Star of Our Union Shines

Underneath the starlit skies,
A promise born that never dies.
Hearts aligned, as one we stand,
Guided by the Lord's own hand.

In every trial, we find grace,
In each other's warm embrace.
Together we shall ever be,
A reflection of divinity.

With faith as our steadfast guide,
In every storm, we shall abide.
Through valleys low and mountains grand,
United in a sacred band.

Let the star of our union gleam,
A guiding light, a vibrant dream.
In harmony, our souls shall sing,
To the joys that love will bring.

Forever bound by sacred ties,
In the warmth of love, our spirits rise.
In faith and trust, we firmly lay,
Our lives as offerings each day.

A Symphony of Sacred Togetherness

In the silence, hearts can hear,
A symphony of love is near.
With every note, our souls ignite,
In sacred dance, we seek the light.

From every struggle, strength we sow,
In unity, our spirits grow.
Harmonies that lift the soul,
In togetherness, we are whole.

Each whisper shared, a loving sound,
In communion, grace is found.
Through laughter, tears, and prayers we weave,
A tapestry of love we believe.

In sacred spaces, time stands still,
With every heartbeat, we fulfill.
The melodies of faith resound,
In every home, love's beauty surrounds.

Together, we shall rise and sing,
Creating joy in everything.
In this symphony, we shall share,
The sacred bond, a love so rare.

Eternal Embrace of Grace

In every moment, grace does flow,
A gentle touch, a soft hello.
In each embrace, a promise made,
Our hearts in love are not afraid.

Through storms that shake the soul's core,
We find the light, we seek for more.
With faith our guide, we rise anew,
In every trial, our love shines through.

In silence shared, our spirits climb,
To heights where love transcends all time.
With every heartbeat, prayer ascends,
In truth, our journey never ends.

In grace, we breathe, in peace, we dwell,
In every story, love will tell.
In sacred rhythms of the heart,
Eternal bonds, we shall impart.

Amidst the chaos of the day,
In love's embrace, we find our way.
With gratitude, we live and grow,
In the grace that we truly know.

Angels Whispering Connection

In silence we hear the softest song,
Angels calling, guiding us along.
A gentle touch that stirs our heart,
In every prayer, we find our part.

An unseen bond, a love profound,
In every moment, grace is found.
Through trials faced, we feel their might,
In shadows cast, they bring us light.

Hope unfolds as wings do soar,
Together in faith, we seek for more.
Each whispered prayer, a sacred thread,
In holy echoes, our spirits are fed.

Connection deepens, forever near,
In every tear, they hold our fear.
Through laughter shared and sorrow's hue,
We find the path that leads us through.

With open hearts, we share our dreams,
In unity, life's river streams.
The angels' whispers never cease,
In their embrace, we find our peace.

The Garden of Our Togetherness

In the garden where love is sown,
Seeds of kindness, gently grown.
Flowers bloom in vibrant grace,
Each petal tells of our embrace.

Sunlight dances on tender leaves,
In this haven, our spirit weaves.
Nourished by trust, rooted in prayer,
In every moment, we linger there.

The fragrance sweet, a holy bond,
In laughter's echo, hearts respond.
Together we tend this sacred ground,
In silence shared, our souls are found.

As seasons shift, we stand as one,
In summer's warmth, or winter's sun.
The garden thrives, in joy and strife,
A testament to our shared life.

With every tear, a river flows,
In joy's embrace, our connection grows.
Through faith we gather, hand in hand,
In this garden, forever we'll stand.

The Threads of Eternal Embrace

Woven softly through time and space,
Threads of love in a warm embrace.
Each moment shared, a stitch so fine,
In the fabric of fate, our hearts entwine.

A tapestry bright, with colors bold,
Stories of faith and dreams untold.
In grief or joy, we find our thread,
With every prayer, our souls are fed.

Yards of hope stretch far and wide,
With every challenge, we turn the tide.
A pattern formed by hands divine,
In unity, our spirits shine.

In twilight's glow, the threads will gleam,
We gather strength to chase the dream.
With every heartbeat, a promise made,
In love's embrace, we won't be swayed.

Through trials faced, together we stand,
Our hearts beat strong, as one we'll band.
The threads of life, forever traced,
In this eternal, sacred space.

Bound by Heaven's Quiet Call

In quiet moments, the heart reveals,
A call from heaven, that gently heals.
Through stillness felt, through whispers known,
In sacred spaces, love is shown.

An echo soft, a soothing balm,
In stormy seas, we find our calm.
Guided by light, a path so clear,
In every doubt, we draw you near.

With open arms, our spirits blend,
In love's embrace, all wounds will mend.
Bonds forged in faith, steadfast, true,
Each step we take, we walk anew.

The call is clear, we shall not stray,
Together through night, we find our day.
In hope's cocoon, we rise and soar,
Bound by heaven, forevermore.

With every breath, we sing our song,
In unity, we all belong.
Through trials faced, our spirits stand,
In heaven's grace, we hold command.

Divine Echoes of Our Togetherness

In the quiet moments, we hear the call,
A sacred bond woven, unbreakable thrall.
Voices in chorus, lifting us high,
In love's soft embrace, together we fly.

With each spoken word, a prayer we weave,
In faith's gentle arms, we learn to believe.
Hearts intertwined, as the heavens decree,
United in purpose, forever we'll be.

Across the valleys, through trials we roam,
Guided by hope, we find our true home.
Each step we take, hand in hand we go,
In the light of His grace, our spirits will grow.

In shadows that linger, His presence is near,
Whispers of guidance, dispelling our fear.
Together we journey, through storms and through peace,
In harmony's song, our souls find release.

The echoes of laughter, the tears that we share,
In the fabric of life, a love always rare.
As we walk this path, with hearts open wide,
Together in spirit, forever our guide.

Faith's Whisper Across the Ages

Through the corridors of time, faith's light shines,
A beacon of hope, in the darkest designs.
Voices of the past, in wisdom they teach,
In the stillness of night, their words softly reach.

Gathered in circles, prayers rise like smoke,
In every soft whisper, the universe spoke.
Together we stand, in belief we abide,
In the warmth of His light, our spirits confide.

Through trials and triumphs, the stories we share,
In the tapestry woven, a love so rare.
Hand in hand, we walk this sacred path,
Together in faith, we shall conquer the wrath.

A tapestry rich with the threads of our quest,
In the depths of our hunger, He knows us best.
With each passing moment, our spirits align,
A legacy written, in love's pure design.

In silence we ponder, in trust we unite,
Guided by the stars that adorn the night.
Faith's whispers endure, across limitless skies,
Together we flourish, where the spirit flies.

Celestial Roots Binding Our Hearts

In the garden of time, our roots intertwine,
A sacred connection, divine and benign.
Together we flourish, through sun and through rain,
In the depths of our souls, love conquers the pain.

Through valleys of sorrow, we still find the way,
With courage ignited, we greet each new day.
In laughter and tears, our bonds become strong,
In the melody of life, together we belong.

The universe speaks in the rustle of leaves,
As the heartache subsides, and the spirit believes.
In the embrace of the stars, our dreams will take flight,
With the light of our love, we illuminate night.

Together we gather, the stories unfold,
In the warmth of our hearth, a love to behold.
United in purpose, our paths ever twine,
Celestial roots, in the cosmos align.

With each heartbeat echoing, a truth we proclaim,
In the tapestry woven, we carry His name.
Bound by the promise of grace from above,
In the dance of our spirits, we flourish in love.

The Light of Togetherness Illuminated

Beneath the vast heavens, where silence resides,
Together we gather, where true love abides.
In the light of His mercy, our hearts come alive,
In unity's glow, we find strength to survive.

Through the whispers of breezes, our prayers ascend,
Each moment we share, a gift we extend.
Within every heartbeat, a rhythm divine,
In togetherness forged, our spirits entwine.

As dawn breaks anew, and shadows take flight,
In the stillness of morning, we bask in the light.
Together we walk, on this path that we share,
Through blessings and burdens, in faith we prepare.

In the rich tapestry of love's sacred dance,
Hand in hand we journey, embracing each chance.
With laughter like sunlight, and tears of pure grace,
In the light of togetherness, we find our place.

In the depths of our souls, a promise resides,
In the circle of life, where true love abides.
Together we shine, as the stars brightly do,
In the light of His love, we are ever anew.

Anchored in the Light of Love

In shadows deep, His love will shine,
A beacon bright, a love divine.
Through storms that rage and trials sore,
We find our peace, we seek no more.

With every heart, a tethered thread,
In sacred trust, where souls are led.
His light within, a guiding star,
In every step, He's never far.

The warmth of grace, like morning sun,
Restores our hope, we are as one.
In whispers soft, His voice we hear,
His presence close, we hold Him dear.

Through valleys low, on mountains high,
In every breath, we live, not die.
Our spirits soar, in unity,
Anchored in love, forever free.

So let us stand, hand in hand as one,
With hearts ablaze, till day is done.
In every life, His light we spread,
Anchored in love, by faith we're led.

A Pilgrim's Path Between Us

A journey shared, we walk in grace,
With every step, we seek His face.
Through winding roads and skies of grey,
Our hearts aligned, we find the way.

Each moment lived, a sacred trust,
In unity, we rise from dust.
With every prayer, a whisper soft,
Together bound, our spirits loft.

Divine embrace, in fellowship,
With open hearts, we share each sip.
The love we give, a seed we sow,
In fields of hope, our spirits grow.

Through trials faced, we bear the load,
Our faith a light upon the road.
In joy and pain, we walk as one,
A pilgrim's path till our days are done.

So hand in hand, we'll greet the dawn,
With thankful hearts, our fears withdrawn.
In every stride, His love enfolds,
A pilgrims' path, with tales retold.

The Communion of Kindred Souls

In gentle whispers, spirits meet,
Awake in love, hearts skip a beat.
A bond unbroken, pure and true,
In sacred space, I find you.

With open arms, we gather near,
In every laugh, we shed a tear.
The ties that bind, a sacred thread,
In communion deep, our spirits led.

In quiet moments, wisdom flows,
A shared embrace where kindness grows.
Through every trial, we stand as one,
In sunset's glow, our race is run.

The love we share, a holy flame,
A tranquil peace, no need for fame.
In every heartbeat, souls entwined,
A tapestry of love we find.

So let us dance in joy and song,
In harmony, where we belong.
Through all of time, and sea and land,
The communion of souls, forever stand.

Threads of Faith Interlaced with Care

In life's embrace, we weave our dreams,
With faith as thread, our spirit gleams.
Each prayer a stitch, in fabric worn,
Together strong, a friendship born.

Through trials faced, we draw so near,
In every loss, we share the tear.
With kindness rich, we lift the veil,
Together, love will never fail.

The grace we share, a sacred art,
With eyes of hope, we play our part.
In laughter sweet and sorrow's song,
Together, we are where we belong.

With every thread, a story spun,
Of faith and love, two hearts as one.
In every moment, loud or rare,
Threads of faith, interlaced with care.

So let us walk, with hands held tight,
Through darkest hours, we'll find the light.
In every stitch, a bond so rare,
Threads of faith, a gift we share.

A Tapestry of Revered Truths

Threads of faith intertwine,
Woven in the fabric divine.
Each story a whisper, a prayer,
In the light, our souls laid bare.

From ancient tomes and scripture vast,
To vibrant hymns, forever cast.
The wisdom shared, a guiding flame,
In unity, we call His name.

In valleys low and mountains high,
We seek the truth that will not die.
In every heart, a sacred spark,
Illuminating the journey's dark.

We gather 'round the sacred fire,
In search of peace, our hearts aspire.
With open hands, we share our peace,
In love's embrace, our worries cease.

So join the dance, the holy shout,
In reverence, we cast our doubt.
Faith is a tapestry to behold,
Threads of compassion, woven bold.

The Altar of Togetherness

Here at the altar, we unite,
With kindred spirits, pure and bright.
In silence, prayers rise like smoke,
In every heart, a sacred cloak.

Hand in hand, we forge our fate,
With love and hope, we elevate.
Together strong, we face the night,
In shared resolve, we find our light.

Around the table, souls align,
With breaking bread, our hearts entwine.
In celebration, let us sing,
The joy that unity can bring.

Through trials, we remain as one,
In life's great dance, we seek the sun.
Connected deeply, woven tight,
In every tear, there blooms delight.

So bring your dreams, your fears, your prayers,
In this sacred space, the spirit shares.
The altar holds our sacred trust,
In love's embrace, we rise, we must.

Hearts Alight in Sacred Union

In every heart, a radiant glow,
A beacon shining through our woe.
In sacred union, love ignites,
Transforming darkness into light.

Together, we tread the path of grace,
With thankful hearts, we seek His face.
In unity, we find our strength,
With bonds of love that know no length.

Through trials faced, our spirits soar,
In compassion, we open the door.
Embracing each soul, we strive to see,
The beauty in our diversity.

As rivers flow to meet the sea,
So too, our hearts will ever be.
In harmony, our song ascends,
A symphony that never ends.

In every prayer, a thread of hope,
We climb the heights, learn how to cope.
In sacred union, hearts alight,
In loving kindness, we find our light.

Echoes of Love in Holy Spaces

In holy spaces, whispers warm,
Guiding souls through every storm.
Echoes of love, a gentle call,
Embracing hearts, we rise, we fall.

In twilight's grace or dawn's first light,
We gather close, igniting bright.
With every prayer, a love resounds,
In sacred silence, truth abounds.

Each moment lived a precious chance,
In faith's embrace, we share our dance.
Through trials faced, with hearts so true,
In every color, we find you.

As petals fall, they nurture ground,
In love's embrace, we're glory-bound.
With every heartbeat, every sigh,
We're woven into the endless sky.

So let us lift our voices high,
In sacred spaces, never shy.
For love is echoed through the years,
In holy spaces, we join our tears.

Graceful Paths on Holy Ground

Upon the sacred earth we tread,
With every step, our hearts are led.
In whispered prayers, the spirits shine,
Together bound, our souls entwine.

The trees reach high, their arms in prayer,
As sunlight kisses, warm and rare.
Each path we walk in gentle grace,
A loving touch, a warm embrace.

We gather here, where faith ignites,
In every heart, the love unites.
The gentle breeze, a soft caress,
Reminds us still, we are blessed.

The stones beneath, they sing the tunes,
Of ancient hopes beneath the moons.
In sacred joy, our spirits soar,
With every step, we seek for more.

In graceful paths, we find our way,
Through trials faced, come what may.
On holy ground, forever stand,
Together, bound, hand in hand.

A Whispered Prayer for Our Bond

In quiet moments, hearts align,
A whispered prayer, a sacred sign.
Together still, we find our way,
In love's embrace, we surely stay.

The stars above, they witness true,
The bond of souls, forever new.
With every heartbeat, softly pound,
In sweet communion, peace is found.

As seasons turn, like tides they ebb,
A gentle touch, our spirits web.
Through trials faced and joys we share,
A whispered prayer, a loving dare.

In laughter bright, in tears that fall,
We lift each other, rise and call.
In sacred trust, our dreams we weave,
With every vow, we still believe.

This bond we hold, a gift divine,
In every moment, love's design.
Through whispered prayers, we fine-tune
A melody as sweet as June.

Illuminated by the Flame of Us

In stillness found, our hearts alight,
Illuminated by the night.
A flickering flame that binds us tight,
In sacred space, we find our sight.

The warmth it spreads, a gentle glow,
A promise made, forever so.
In every glance, the truth conveyed,
Our love, a path that won't ever fade.

As shadows dance, our spirits rise,
In unity, our voices prize.
Through fiery trails, together roam,
In every heartbeat, we find home.

With open arms, we greet the day,
As warmth surrounds, in faith we sway.
Our love ignites, a beacon bright,
Through trials faced, we claim the light.

Illuminated, hand in hand,
A journey blessed, a promised land.
In sacred space, forever trust,
Our hearts will sing; it's love, it's us.

The Exchange of Love in Sacred Spaces

In sacred spaces, love is shared,
Each glance a gift, a dream declared.
In whispered words, our souls connect,
In every heartbeat, we reflect.

A gentle touch, a tender gaze,
In quiet moments, hearts ablaze.
Through trials faced and laughter sweet,
In love's embrace, our spirits meet.

As seasons change, our vow remains,
In sacred joy, through joys and pains.
With every rise, with every fall,
In love's soft echo, we stand tall.

The silence speaks, our hearts engaged,
In every moment, love's displayed.
Together strong, through thick and thin,
In sacred dance, our souls begin.

In every breath, we find the grace,
The exchange of love, our holy place.
Together bound, our paths entwined,
In sacred spaces, love enshrined.

Graceful Reverence for Each Other

In the stillness of the night,
We find our souls entwined,
A gentle touch, a loving prayer,
In grace our hearts aligned.

Through trials we may walk as one,
In shadows cast by light,
With voices raised to heavens high,
Our spirits in His sight.

With every word that we bestow,
We cherish the divine,
In mutual respect we grow,
With patience, love, and time.

Each moment shared, each tear we shed,
Is woven in His plan,
In reverence for one another,
We boldly take His hand.

Together we shall rise and shine,
In harmony we lift,
With hearts in motion, souls refined,
In His embrace, our gift.

Heartstrings Woven by Divine Hands

In the tapestry of our lives,
Threads of joy and pain,
With every heartbeat we survive,
In love we'll remain.

Each note within the sacred hymn,
Is played with tender grace,
A symphony of light within,
Where every soul finds place.

With faith, our paths converge anew,
In light of love's embrace,
Where heartstrings weave a bond so true,
In God's eternal space.

Through trials faced, together strong,
With courage side by side,
We'll sing the ancient, hopeful song,
In Him, we shall abide.

By sacred hands our lives entwined,
In unity we stand,
A melody both rare and kind,
In God's eternal plan.

The Quilt of Togetherness and Faith

In every square of patchwork bright,
A story finds its home,
With threads of love to warm the night,
Together we shall roam.

With faith as needle, prayer as thread,
We stitch our lives as one,
In every moment, joy once spread,
Is woven, never done.

Through seasons change, our hearts will grow,
With every tear and smile,
In love's embrace, we come to know,
Together, all the while.

The quilt shall hold our dreams and fears,
With patterns rich and deep,
Each tapestry a blend of years,
A promise we shall keep.

In faith we find our strength combined,
In unity, we're strong,
This quilt of life, in love defined,
Is where our hearts belong.

In the Palm of Celestial Whisper

In silence soft, the whispers flow,
A love that knows no end,
Guiding us where we must go,
In faith, our hearts we lend.

With every breath, a prayer ascends,
In harmony we rise,
With trust that all our journey bends,
In light beneath the skies.

Embraced within His gentle hand,
We find our resting place,
In grace, together we shall stand,
In His warmth, His face.

Through storms that shake our very core,
We learn to dance in strife,
With every trial we explore,
We cherish gifted life.

In whispers soft, we hear His call,
Together, hand in hand,
In the palm of love, we stand tall,
As part of His great plan.

Whispers of the Spirit's Bond

In the silence, spirits speak,
A gentle touch, a light so meek.
Guided hearts in sacred trust,
Together we rise, as love is a must.

In each prayer, our souls align,
Echoes soft, in faith we shine.
Bound by grace, our fears released,
In His love, our hearts find peace.

Through trials we walk, hand in hand,
In the light of the promised land.
Whispers of hope like stars above,
Illuminating the path of love.

With every tear, a lesson learned,
In the fire of love, we've burned.
Together we dance, a divine embrace,
In the spirit's bond, we find our place.

Cherished Moments Under Heaven

In the twilight, whispers bloom,
Cherished moments dispel the gloom.
Hearts entwined, a sacred blend,
A glimpse of grace, our spirits mend.

Under heaven's watchful gaze,
We find joy in simple ways.
A laugh, a sigh, a soft caress,
In love's embrace, we find our rest.

From the dawn till stars ignite,
Your hand in mine feels so right.
In every laugh, in every tear,
I see your soul and hold it dear.

Through valleys low and mountains high,
Faithful hearts will never die.
With every moment, grace displays,
In cherished time, we find our praise.

Together, we weave a tapestry bright,
In love's warm glow, we find the light.
Forever grateful, our spirits soar,
In every heartbeat, we seek for more.

Eternal Vows of Unity

In the presence of love divine,
Eternal vows in a sacred line.
With spirit and heart, we make our stand,
In unity's grasp, we weave our hand.

Promised whispers in the night,
Joining souls, a heavenly sight.
In every pledge, a story told,
In love's embrace, we break the mold.

Through every storm, we shall not part,
In every beat, we share one heart.
With open arms, we gather grace,
In eternal vows, we find our place.

With faith unyielding, we rise anew,
In every challenge, our love stays true.
A union blessed, forever strong,
Together, we sing our lifelong song.

In unity, we find our way,
Each moment a gift, come what may.
Hand in hand, we seek the light,
In eternal vows, our spirits unite.

Celestial Hands Intertwined

In the quiet, hands entwined,
Divine connection, hearts aligned.
With gentle grace, we face the dawn,
In sacred love, our fears are gone.

Each touch a prayer, each gaze a song,
In celestial bond, where we belong.
With open hearts, the world will see,
In unity's light, we are free.

From starlit skies to earthly ground,
In love's embrace, we are spellbound.
Through trials faced, no need to hide,
In faith's embrace, we shall abide.

As seasons change, our roots run deep,
In dream and hope, our promises keep.
Together we walk, hand in hand,
In celestial love, forever we stand.

With every breath, we seek the truth,
In softest whispers, we find our youth.
Celestial hands, forever twined,
In this journey, our hearts defined.

In the Sanctuary of Our Souls

In stillness, we gather close,
Hearts aligned in silent prayer,
Veils of doubt gently lifted,
In the light, we find our care.

The whispers of grace surround,
Comfort in each gentle breath,
A refuge in sacred sound,
Where love conquers all, even death.

In this hallowed place of peace,
Each soul binds in unity,
Embracing divine release,
Finding strength in humility.

Together we rise, hands entwined,
Through trials and storms we stand,
With faith as the thread that binds,
A tapestry woven by His hand.

In the sanctuary, we are one,
With joy our spirits ignite,
Transcending all shadows spun,
In love's ever-constant light.

Faithful Threads of Togetherness

In the fabric of our days,
Stitches of warmth interlace,
Through trials and hopeful praise,
We find strength in love's embrace.

Each thread tells a story dear,
Of journeys walked, hand in hand,
Calming every whispered fear,
In faith, together we stand.

Through valleys low, on mountains high,
We share burdens, joys, and tears,
With each laugh and every sigh,
A covenant spans the years.

As stars bound in heaven's dome,
Shining bright in darkest night,
With every heart, we build a home,
Where love forever takes flight.

In unity, we find our grace,
Each moment a sacred thread,
In the dance of time and space,
Together, hand in hand, we tread.

Embracing the Divine Embrace

In the stillness of our hearts,
We reach for the heavens high,
With open arms, love imparts,
A sacred bond that will not die.

The breath of the Spirit flows,
Filling spaces pure and bright,
In each moment, revelation grows,
Illuminating shadows with light.

As petals seek the sun's warm grace,
We turn toward the divine call,
In the surrender, we find our place,
In His arms, we rise, we fall.

With faith as our armor strong,
We walk this path hand in hand,
A melody of love's sweet song,
Guided by His gentle hand.

In every embrace, sacred and bold,
We find solace, we find peace,
In the love that we behold,
Every fear and doubt shall cease.

Ties Woven in Sacred Light

In the loom of divine design,
Threads of life entwine as one,
Creating patterns, pure and fine,
In harmony, our hearts are spun.

With each moment, a weave takes flight,
Binding souls in love's great cause,
Through trials faced, we find our might,
In the beauty of this divine pause.

In the tapestry of shared grace,
We unfurl our dreams and fears,
Embracing each other's sacred space,
A sanctuary through the years.

With threads of hope, we stitch anew,
Each knot a promise made in love,
A guide through dark, a path so true,
As we journey toward above.

Together, we rise, hearts ignited,
In the glow of the sacred light,
Bound by love, forever united,
In the presence of His might.

The Mirrored Paths of Trust and Love

In realms where faith does grow,
Two paths converge, they softly glow.
Hand in hand, we tread this way,
In trust and love, we find our stay.

Beneath the stars, our hearts take flight,
Guided by the sacred light.
Together we shall face the storm,
In every trial, our hope is warm.

Like rivers flow, our spirits meld,
In whispered prayers, the truth upheld.
The mirrored paths that we must walk,
In silence sweet, our hearts will talk.

With every step, we share our song,
A melody where we belong.
In love's embrace, we find our grace,
A timeless bond that none can erase.

Our Soul's Journey Intertwined in Light

In the tapestry of fate, we weave,
Threads of hope that never leave.
Our souls dance under heavens bright,
Together bound by love and light.

In shadows cast, our spirits soar,
Eclipsing doubts that were before.
Each moment shared, a sacred gift,
In union strong, our spirits lift.

Through valleys deep and mountains high,
We seek the truth beneath the sky.
Our journey marked by grace divine,
In every heartbeat, your heart's mine.

With open arms, we greet the dawn,
A promise made, a love reborn.
In faith's embrace, we find our way,
Illuminated by love's ray.

Embraced by Divine Providence

In every breath, a blessing falls,
A gentle whisper that softly calls.
Through trials faced, we're never lost,
In love's embrace, we bear the cost.

The hands of fate, they guide our stride,
With grace and mercy, right beside.
In every storm, we find our peace,
With faith, our worries find release.

The light of dawn breaks through the night,
Revealing paths with promises bright.
In every heart, a sacred song,
Encouraging us to carry on.

Connected deep by unseen ties,
In love's pure depths, our spirit flies.
We trust the way, we trust the hour,
Embraced forever by His power.

The Legacy of Love's Touch

From ancient roots, our story grows,
A legacy that softly flows.
In loving hands, the warmth of grace,
Each gentle touch a sacred space.

In every laugh, in every tear,
The echoes of our hearts draw near.
Through trials faced, we stand as one,
Together shining like the sun.

With every step upon this land,
We leave a mark, a guiding hand.
In whispered dreams, our hopes align,
Two souls entwined in love divine.

The legacy we build each day,
In kindness shown along our way.
For in this life, our love will grow,
Its seeds will scatter, freely sow.

Our Hands, Forged in Creation's Plan

Our hands are tools of grace,
We shape the world with care.
In unity we find our place,
Together, hearts laid bare.

With gentle touch, we heal our land,
In every act, love grows.
Crafted by the Father's hand,
In our work, His spirit flows.

Through trials faced and mountains climbed,
We learn the sacred art.
With every struggle, hope entwined,
Forging strength within the heart.

The light of faith, our guiding star,
Illuminates the night.
Though journeys often feel afar,
We walk in love's pure light.

With hands uplifted, prayer ascends,
To realms where mercy reigns.
Together bound, our spirit mends,
In joy, our soul remains.

In the Heart of Divine Closeness

In quiet stillness, spirits meet,
A whisper of the soul's deep plea.
Divine presence, pure and sweet,
In every breath, our hearts agree.

We see His face in every tear,
In laughter shared, in love's embrace.
He walks beside us, always near,
A guiding hand in time and space.

Each moment spent in sacred trust,
We find the peace that love unveils.
A bond unbroken, kind and just,
In faith, our spirit never fails.

In prayer, our voices lift the day,
United hearts in song ascend.
The light of hope will find a way,
In closeness, love knows no end.

In the silence, wisdom grows,
A garden tended by His grace.
In our hearts, the river flows,
Of love that time cannot erase.

The Pilgrimage of Souls Entwined

In every step, a story told,
Together through this sacred land.
With faith as guide, our journey bold,
We walk united, hand in hand.

Each soul a note in harmony,
In melodies both sweet and true.
Through valleys deep and mountains free,
We rise with hope, refreshed anew.

The path is steep, yet love will shine,
A beacon on the darkest nights.
In trials faced, our spirits twine,
Forever bound in sacred lights.

Each heart a lantern, bright and clear,
Illuminating all we find.
Together facing every fear,
With trust that love will be our kind.

The pilgrimage leads ever on,
With lessons learned and joy regained.
In every sunset, we are drawn,
To share the love that won't be drained.

Love's Testament Carved in Time

In every heartbeat, love's refrain,
A testament we hold so dear.
Through countless struggles, loss, and gain,
In heart's embrace, we conquer fear.

With every tear, a story weeped,
In joy and sorrow, life's true art.
Love's legacy is richly steeped,
In the depths of each loving heart.

The hands that serve, the hearts that guide,
In service, grace begins to bloom.
Through acts of kindness, love's abide,
We find the light that breaks the gloom.

Each moment shared, a precious gem,
In the tapestry, woven tight.
Love leaves its mark, and we condemn
The shadows fled by purest light.

As seasons change and years unfold,
Love's testament shall ever shine.
In every story, truth retold,
We live, we love, in His design.

Love's Pilgrimage Through Time

In the dawn of creation, we roam,
With hearts intertwined, seeking our home.
Through valleys of sorrow, to peaks of grace,
Each step a testament, to Love's embrace.

Winds whisper stories, of ages gone by,
Echoes of kindness, beneath the sky.
In moments of struggle, our spirits align,
For in every trial, we find Love divine.

The rivers of faith, they flow deep and wide,
Carving our souls, with the love we can't hide.
Through laughter and tears, we navigate fate,
In patience and courage, our hearts resonate.

Embracing the journey, hand in hand we tread,
With visions of peace, on Love's path ahead.
From shadows to light, our spirits we bring,
In unity's bond, we eternally sing.

At twilight of life, when the stars appear,
We'll gather together, with hearts sincere.
In the essence of time, Love's truth we'll find,
For every pilgrimage is Love intertwined.

The Light of Presence in Every Breath

In silence we gather, our hearts start to hum,
The breath of the universe whispers, 'Come.'
In the depth of the moment, calmness is found,
A sacred connection, where grace does abound.

Each inhale invites the divine into sight,
With exhale, we share the profound, pure light.
In rhythms of being, our spirits align,
With Love's gentle echo, our souls intertwine.

Through trials and triumphs, we seek and we learn,
In the fire of presence, our hearts brightly burn.
Each heartbeat a hymn, a prayer softly said,
With gratitude rising, our spirits are fed.

In gathering stillness, we find ourselves whole,
With the Light of presence illuminating our souls.
In every breath taken, a canvas is drawn,
Of love everlasting, from dusk until dawn.

In the tapestry woven of laughter and tears,
We paint our devotion through all of our years.
In unity's grace, let our spirits take flight,
In the warmth of Love's presence, we bask in the light.

Pilgrims in the Landscape of Affection

Upon the great canvas, we carve out our name,
As pilgrims of Love, we play this vast game.
In valleys of longing, on mountains of trust,
We wander as seekers, with hearts filled with lust.

Through pathways of kindness, our spirits we weave,
In each thread of connection, together we cleave.
With laughter that dances on sun-kissed terrain,
In the garden of affection, we flourish again.

The rivers of empathy flow deep in our veins,
In the storms of compassion, we weather the pains.
In moments of sharing, our burdens grow light,
For Love is the lantern that guides us through night.

In the fields of existence, where hearts intertwine,
Every step of our journey is lovingly divine.
As pilgrims we cherish the beauty we find,
In the landscape of affection, where souls are aligned.

With each sacred heartbeat, we nurture our ties,
In the warmth of each other, our spirit does rise.
The pilgrimage endless, for Love knows no end,
Hand in hand we journey, forever as friends.

Unity in the Silence of Prayer

In the hush of the morning, our spirits arise,
In the stillness of prayer, we reach for the skies.
With hearts open wide, we whisper our dreams,
In the unity found, pure love softly gleams.

Through shadows of doubt, our faith becomes bright,
As candles of hope flicker, igniting the night.
In moments of silence, our souls intertwine,
For in every still breath, we feel the divine.

Together we gather, in circles of grace,
In the presence of love, we each find our place.
With gratitude swelling, our hearts beat as one,
In the silence of prayer, all battles are won.

Through challenges faced, with hands held up high,
We rise like the dawn, painting colors in sky.
With love as our anchor, we stand side by side,
In the unity of prayer, our spirits abide.

In the tapestry woven, in stitches of care,
We find in each other, the truth that we share.
In the silence of prayer, let our souls take flight,
For united in Love, we are one with the Light.

A Sanctuary Built on Love's Promise

In the quiet of dawn, hope does arise,
Whispers of grace reach the skies.
Together we stand, hand in hand,
A refuge of peace in this blessed land.

With faith as our guide, hearts open wide,
In love's gentle arms, we abide.
Trusting the path that is laid ahead,
In the warmth of His presence, we are fed.

Each prayer a flower, blooming anew,
Roots intertwined in the morning dew.
In shadows of doubt, His light we seek,
In the strength of our bond, we find our peak.

Through trials we journey, together we rise,
Embracing the truth, we open our eyes.
For this sanctuary is built on His grace,
In the heart of our love, we find our place.

The Garden Where Hearts Flourish

In the garden where silence speaks,
Every petal of faith, a promise it keeps.
With roots that reach deep, our spirits unite,
In the warmth of His love, we shine bright.

Beneath the sun's gaze, our dreams take flight,
Nurtured by kindness, we grow in His light.
Each seed of compassion, carefully sown,
Blossoms in hearts that are lovingly grown.

The fragrance of hope fills the air,
As we tend to each other with fervent care.
Direction from heaven guides our way,
In the garden of grace, we choose to stay.

Through storms and trials, we weather the night,
In the promise of dawn, we find our sight.
Together we flourish, nourished by love,
As we walk hand in hand, guided from above.

Miracles of Togetherness Amidst Trials

In the depths of struggle, we hold each other,
Finding strength in the bond of sister and brother.
United we stand, hearts brave and true,
Through the trials that life brings, we still pursue.

Each challenge a chapter, a lesson to learn,
In the fire of faith, our spirits do burn.
Side by side, through shadows we roam,
In the warmth of His mercy, we find our home.

Miracles blossom when hope feels remote,
In prayers of love, our spirits devote.
Together we journey, hand in hand,
With trust in His plan, we firmly stand.

With every hardship, our hearts grow wide,
For in this togetherness, love is our guide.
Miracles of kindness weave through the night,
As we walk in faith, our souls take flight.

Walking in Faith's Gentle Embrace

In the stillness of night, we tread with grace,
Feeling the warmth of faith's embrace.
With each step we take, peace fills the air,
Guided by love, we find solace there.

The path may twist, with shadows to face,
But in heart's quiet whispers, we find our place.
His light shines softly, dispelling the dark,
In every heartbeat, we find the spark.

Through valleys of doubt, our spirits are kissed,
In the promise of joy, we find none to miss.
Hand in hand, we walk this road,
In the grace of His love, we lighten the load.

Together we sing, in harmony's song,
In faith's gentle arms, we forever belong.
With eyes fixed on heaven, we rise above,
Walking in peace, wrapped in His love.

Between the Divine and the Beloved

In whispers soft, the spirit sighs,
A love that blooms beyond the skies.
With hands held high, we seek the grace,
Of sacred bonds in this holy space.

Each prayer a star in the vast expanse,
Guiding our hearts in a timeless dance.
In unity we rise, spirits aligned,
Finding the light that love defined.

Through trials faced, like rivers wide,
We tread together, side by side.
In each heartbeat, a promise made,
In every glance, our fears allayed.

The love divine, a gentle guide,
In every tear, He is our pride.
Through valleys low and mountains high,
His presence lingers, ever nigh.

So let us walk, hand in hand,
Through sacred dreams upon this land.
In every moment, let love reign,
As we find bliss in joy and pain.

Sacred Steps Taken Side by Side

In the shadows where silence dwells,
We walk together, hear wisdom's bells.
Each step we take, a prayer unfurls,
As sacred light within us swirls.

With faith our shield, we forge ahead,
In love's embrace, no need for dread.
Trust in the journey, hearts entwined,
In every hug, our souls aligned.

Each moment shared, a treasure grown,
In the garden of love, we are not alone.
With joyous hearts, we greet the dawn,
In sacred steps, a bond reborn.

Through storm and calm, our spirits soar,
Hand in hand, we seek to explore.
In every heartbeat, a song of praise,
In each other's eyes, the divine displays.

Let us rejoice, our voices rise,
In harmony beneath the skies.
Together onward, forever we'll glide,
In faith and love, side by side.

Bonds of Light in Life's Journey

In the tapestry of life, we weave,
Threads of golden light that never leave.
In every moment, a story told,
Through trials faced and joys behold.

As daylight fades and shadows creep,
In faith's embrace, we find our keep.
Our souls entwined, like vines that climb,
Reaching for heaven, transcending time.

With every heartbeat, a sacred beat,
In love's embrace, we find our seat.
Together we journey through thick and thin,
With hearts united, we shall win.

In the echoes of prayer, we find our peace,
Every doubt released, our worries cease.
As starlight guides us through the night,
We'll walk in faith, our spirits bright.

So take my hand, let's brave the storm,
In our connection, we are reborn.
With bonds of light, together we'll soar,
Finding the grace forevermore.

The Unseen Bond of Our Spirits

In stillness deep, our spirits meet,
A silent whisper, our hearts repeat.
With open arms, love's truth unfolds,
In the warmth of kindness, our story molds.

Though paths may part, and seasons change,
The bond we share will never estrange.
Through every trial, we persevere,
The unseen bond, forever clear.

Like stars that shine in the darkest night,
Our spirits dance in the pale moonlight.
In every moment, a touch divine,
In every heartbeat, your soul is mine.

Through joy and sorrow, we find our way,
In love's embrace, come what may.
Together we'll rise, like the morning sun,
In faith and trust, we are as one.

So let our spirits forever entwine,
In sacred moments, love is defined.
In the journey ahead, let grace consume,
For in this bond, our hearts will bloom.

Celestial Shadows Dancing Together

In the stillness, stars align,
A dance of shadows, divine.
Each whisper shared in twilight glow,
Connecting hearts, as rivers flow.

Moonlit paths where spirits roam,
Guiding us to our eternal home.
In the embrace of sacred night,
We find our truth, our inner light.

Together we rise, on wings of grace,
In celestial realms, we find our place.
With every heartbeat, we draw near,
Casting aside all doubt and fear.

Each moment shared, a holy thread,
Binding souls, where angels tread.
As shadows twine, we take our stand,
In the circle of the sacred band.

Through the silence, love will thrive,
In the dance of life, we are alive.
Celestial shadows, hand in hand,
We weave our dreams across the land.

The Heartbeat of Us in Sacred Silence

In the hush, our spirits sing,
Quiet prayers, the joy they bring.
With each heartbeat, grace unfolds,
A tapestry of love, it molds.

In sacred silence, we unite,
Finding solace in the night.
Each breath a hymn, pure and true,
Reflecting the essence of me and you.

In the stillness, love does bloom,
Banishing shadows, dispelling gloom.
Together we rise, through thick and thin,
In this sacred space, we begin.

The heartbeat echoes, soft yet loud,
In shadows cast, beneath the cloud.
With open hearts, we share our song,
In the sacred silence, we belong.

Let us cherish this blessed hour,
In the depths of love, we find our power.
With gratitude, our souls entwine,
In sacred silence, divine design.

Hymns of Unity Beneath Heaven's Canopy

Beneath the vast, unending sky,
We lift our voices, letting fly.
Hymns of unity, resound and soar,
In every heart, an open door.

Under heaven's watchful gaze,
We find our strength in love's embrace.
Each note a promise, pure and sweet,
A melody where spirits meet.

Together we rise, in harmony,
Filling the air with our reverie.
Every echo joins the throng,
In the symphony of right and wrong.

Hearts entwined, our spirits dance,
In the light of faith, we take our chance.
With every breath, the song prevails,
Uniting us where love unveils.

Let our hymns be the bridge we build,
In every soul, the void is filled.
Under heaven's canopy, we sing,
In unity, the joy we bring.

In the Quietude of Divine Togetherness

In the quietude, we find our peace,
A moment shared, where worries cease.
With whispered prayers, we touch the sky,
In divine togetherness, we fly.

Softly spoken, heartbeats blend,
In gentle silence, we transcend.
Our spirits merge, as rivers stream,
In the stillness, we softly dream.

Together we bask in sacred light,
Navigating shadows, taking flight.
In every glance, a deepened trust,
With love as our bond, we must.

In this quiet space, souls ignite,
Illuminated by love's pure light.
Every sigh, a testament true,
In the divine, we begin anew.

Let us linger in this gentle grace,
Finding solace in our embrace.
In quietude, we're never apart,
Joined in the dance of each other's heart.

Love's Covenant Written in the Stars

In twilight's glow, the promise burns,
Heaven weaves the tales we learn.
Whispers soft as the night breeze,
Hearts entwined, our spirits ease.

Beneath the moon, our fears take flight,
Guided by the stars so bright.
In sacred bonds, our journey starts,
With faith and love, we share our hearts.

Each twinkle holds a vow sincere,
Echoing love that draws us near.
Together in this vast expanse,
We dance, we dream, we take our chance.

Through storms and calm, we shall endure,
With every heartbeat, love is pure.
In the cosmic stretch, our souls align,
A covenant formed, eternally divine.

In the silence, our prayers rise,
Carried forth to the endless skies.
Forever etched in starlit gleam,
A love that's more than just a dream.

The Sanctuary of Shared Breath

In sacred space where souls converge,
With every sigh, our hearts emerge.
A sanctuary, soft and warm,
Protecting love from any harm.

Hands held tight in gentle grace,
Reflecting light on every face.
In harmony, we find our song,
Where every note reminds us strong.

Eyes that speak of ancient tales,
In whispered winds, our spirit sails.
Together in this hallowed ground,
Eternal love's sweet voice is found.

With breaths entwined, we share the air,
Creating moments, rich and rare.
In this space, our shadows blend,
As we journey and transcend.

In unity, we rise above,
Embracing all that we hold dear.
In the sanctuary of shared breath,
We celebrate life, conquer death.

Unity Found in Graceful Shadows

In twilight's veil, two shadows play,
Dancing softly at the end of day.
Hand in hand, we tread the line,
In every step, our hearts align.

Underneath the trees so tall,
Whispers linger, a gentle call.
In secret glades where dreams reside,
We find the truth that worlds abide.

In every shadow, love's embrace,
Graceful movements, a tender trace.
Two souls united, never apart,
A melody etched upon the heart.

As stars emerge to light our way,
Hope ignites in the fading gray.
With gratitude, we share this space,
Unity shines on every face.

In moments quiet, joy unfolds,
Binding tales that love upholds.
In graceful shadows, we refine,
A sacred bond, forever divine.

Eternal Flames of Shared Devotion

In the hearth of love, flames arise,
Brighter than the morning skies.
A fire that warms, ignites the soul,
In its glow, we find our whole.

Each flicker tells a story clear,
Of joy, of hurt, of laughter dear.
Together, we fuel the sacred fire,
With every glance, our hearts inspire.

In the winds of time, our embers sway,
Boundless love guides our way.
Through trials faced, and nights so long,
In shared devotion, we grow strong.

A flame that dances, wild and free,
Reflecting hopes for you and me.
In each heartbeat, we find the light,
Eternal flames banish the night.

Together, we tend this holy spark,
Illuminating paths through dark.
In devotion's glow, we shall remain,
Eternal flames that will not wane.

Sacred Threads of Connection

In quiet moments, we seek your grace,
A tapestry woven, in sacred space.
Threads of love, entwined with care,
Guiding our hearts, your presence there.

With every breath, our spirits rise,
Illuminated by your holy skies.
Hands held together, in prayer we stand,
United in faith, throughout the land.

Your whispers echo, in gentle streams,
We walk in faith, fulfilling dreams.
In every heart, your light shall shine,
A sacred thread, forever divine.

Together we flourish, in harmony's dance,
Fostering hope, in a world of chance.
With open hearts, we share our plight,
And find our way in your guiding light.

These sacred threads, connect us all,
In times of joy and when we fall.
Bound by love, we lift our voice,
In unity, we make our choice.

Cherished Bonds in Celestial Light

Beneath the stars, your love we find,
A bond so strong, forever entwined.
In every heartbeat, your wisdom flows,
In cherished moments, our spirit grows.

Hands raised in prayer, we seek your face,
Finding solace in every trace.
With faith as our anchor, we stand tall,
Bound by love's gentle, beckoning call.

Through trials and tests, your grace remains,
A guiding light in our darkest pains.
In unity, we find our way,
In celestial light, forever to stay.

The ties of love, like stars align,
Shining brightly, truly divine.
Each heart a beacon, in love's embrace,
Together we gather, in sacred space.

Cherished bonds in your name we weave,
In every soul, your gifts, believe.
A chorus of hope, across the night,
In celestial dreams, we take our flight.

The Ties That Prayer Has Weaved

In whispered prayer, our spirits rise,
Connecting hearts beneath the skies.
With every word, a sacred thread,
In faith we journey, where angels tread.

Through trials faced and burdens borne,
The ties of prayer, forever worn.
In moments of doubt, we find our peace,
Through every struggle, your love won't cease.

Together we gather, our voices strong,
In harmony's chorus, we belong.
With gratitude deep, we lift our song,
The ties that prayer has woven long.

In every heartbeat, your light does dwell,
A whispered promise, a sacred spell.
Bonds of compassion, in unity's grace,
In the warmth of love, we find our place.

With prayer as our binding, we journey forth,
In every step, we revel in worth.
Hearts intertwined, through joy and strife,
In prayer's embrace, we find our life.

In the Hollow of Divine Presence

In the hollow of your divine embrace,
We seek the solace, the sacred space.
With every heartbeat, your love we feel,
In quiet moments, our souls are healed.

The echo of prayer, a gentle guide,
With each whispered wish, you stand beside.
Through every shadow, your light remains,
In the hollow of trust, love sustains.

As stars align in the midnight glow,
Your grace surrounds us, gently we flow.
In unity's bond, we rise and sing,
In the hollow of faith, our spirits take wing.

With hands lifted high, our hearts released,
In sacred love, our souls find peace.
Embraced by your light, we carry on,
In the hollow of presence, forever drawn.

Together we wander, through valleys deep,
In the company of love, our promises keep.
In every prayer uttered, your presence found,
In the hollow of truth, forever bound.

Sacred Footsteps on Shared Ground

In the silence of morning's grace,
We gather in love's warm embrace.
With whispers of hope, our hearts align,
On sacred paths where spirits shine.

Each step we take in shared delight,
Illuminated by faith's pure light.
Together we walk, in trust we stand,
United in spirit, hand in hand.

With humility, we tread this earth,
Finding wisdom in every birth.
Together we rise, as one we soar,
In the boundless love we explore.

Through trials faced and burdens shared,
In every moment, we're deeply cared.
The echoes of joy sweetly resound,
In the sacred footsteps on shared ground.

Let hearts commune beneath the sky,
In gratitude's song, let voices fly.
Together we kindle the flames of peace,
In unity's strength, we find release.

Tethered by Faith's Embrace

In the stillness of a whispered prayer,
We find each other, beyond despair.
With hands held tight, we face the storm,
Embraced by faith, our hearts grow warm.

The tapestry of life we weave,
In love and hope, we do believe.
Through shadows cast, our spirits lift,
In faith's embrace, we find our gift.

With every trial that we endure,
The bond of love remains so pure.
In the sacred space where we confide,
Together we walk, side by side.

As stars align in the darkest night,
We shine collectively, a perfect light.
In harmony, our voices blend,
In this journey of love, we transcend.

Tethered by faith, we journey far,
Guided by grace, our guiding star.
With hearts as one, we rise above,
In the warm embrace of lasting love.

Cherished Souls in the Light

In the glimmer of love's gentle glow,
We gather together, hearts aglow.
Each soul shines bright, a beacon clear,
Cherished in faith, we hold each dear.

With laughter and tears, our stories blend,
In joyful moments, we find our mend.
As the sun sets on this tranquil plain,
In cherished souls, no love is in vain.

Through the trials that life may send,
Together we stand, hand in hand we bend.
In the dance of life, we rise and fall,
In each other's arms, we find our call.

The light of kindness guides our way,
In every moment, let love stay.
Together we lift each other high,
As cherished souls, together we fly.

With open hearts, we greet the dawn,
In the bond of love, we are reborn.
In this sacred light, we find our place,
As cherished souls, we seek His grace.

The Bond of Grace on This Journey

In the tapestry of life we tread,
We weave our dreams, where angels led.
In every moment, grace unfolds,
In the stories of the loved and bold.

As paths entwine, our spirits soar,
With kindness and love, we explore.
The bond of grace, a sacred art,
In every beat of a loving heart.

With gratitude as our guiding thread,
We honor the words that love has said.
In the richness of each shared glance,
We find our purpose, a sacred dance.

Through trials and triumphs, we will stand,
In the grace of love, we lend a hand.
With open souls, we sing our song,
In the bond of grace, we all belong.

So let us journey, come what may,
Together we grow, by love's sweet sway.
In this embrace, let our hearts be free,
In the bond of grace, we find unity.

Together Under the Watchful Skies

In the twilight's gentle glow,
We gather 'neath heaven's eyes,
Hand in hand, our spirits flow,
United under watchful skies.

Each star a whisper, softly speaks,
Of love that binds our hearts as one,
Together strong, in faith we seek,
The light of grace, our daily sun.

With every prayer, our voices rise,
A chorus sweet in sacred tone,
In harmony, our hopes arise,
Together, never more alone.

The heavens arch, a loving dome,
As we walk this sacred track,
In trust we find our final home,
With souls entwined, no turning back.

So let us shine, with hearts ablaze,
With faith that conquers every fear,
Together in our joyful praise,
We find our purpose, bright and clear.

The Promised Path of Togetherness

Upon the road where shadows play,
We tread with faith, hand in hand,
The promised path that lights our way,
A journey blessed, forever planned.

Each step we take, a sacred gift,
In unity, we walk as one,
Through trials faced, our spirits lift,
In love's embrace, we are reborn.

With every heartbeat drawing near,
The whispers of the Holy guide,
In times of doubt, we cast out fear,
Together strong, forever tied.

This bond we share, so pure, divine,
In every moment, grace abounds,
A tapestry of hearts that shine,
In togetherness, our joy resounds.

So let our spirits joyfully soar,
With faith that carries us above,
On this promised path we explore,
Together, anchored in His love.

Hearts Interwoven in God's Design

In the fabric of His grand design,
Our hearts are woven, thread by thread,
In love's warm glow, a sacred sign,
A tapestry where hope is spread.

As branches cling to sturdy trunks,
We find our strength in every prayer,
Through storms and trials, faith rebunks,
In unity, we cast our care.

With every moment, hand in hand,
Together, facing life's sweet song,
In God's embrace, we firmly stand,
As one in heart, we all belong.

With laughter shared and tears embraced,
In every joy and every strife,
In His bright light, we find our place,
Interwoven threads of love and life.

So let us cherish what we share,
Hearts interwoven, side by side,
In every breath, a fervent prayer,
In love, our spirits choose to glide.

In the Hands of the Divine

In every moment, we are held,
In hands of love, so pure, so kind,
Through trials faced, our hearts compelled,
In the embrace of the divine.

With faith as bright as morning light,
We walk the path of grace anew,
Together shining, day and night,
In every step, His love rings true.

In whispered prayers, our spirits soar,
With gratitude, our hearts align,
In every challenge, we implore,
To trust and rest in hands divine.

As rivers flow, our lives entwined,
In harmony, we sing His praise,
With joy and peace, our hearts designed,
In each embrace, His love displays.

So let us dance in sacred grace,
In hands of the divine, we stand,
With love unwavering, we embrace,
Together bound, by God's own hand.

The Chorus of Our Souls

In the silence, we gather in prayer,
Voices rising, filling the air.
Hearts entwined in sacred song,
Together we stand, forever strong.

With each note, a story unfolds,
Of faith unyielding, and love that molds.
Through trials faced, our spirits soar,
In unity, we seek evermore.

A melody sweet, harmonies blend,
A chorus of hope, on which we depend.
In whispers of grace, we journey ahead,
Bound by the truths that our hearts have said.

From mountains high to valleys low,
Our voices unite, a radiant glow.
Together we rise, like stars in the night,
Illuminating paths with heavenly light.

In the song of our souls, let echo resound,
For in love's embrace, our purpose is found.
With each heartfelt note, let praises arise,
A chorus unbroken, ascending the skies.

Beneath the Canopy of Grace

Under the branches of mercy we stand,
Lost in the beauty of God's gentle hand.
With every leaf that whispers and sways,
We find our peace in the divine rays.

In the shade of compassion, we seek to connect,
Bound by the love that we choose to respect.
The fruits of our labor blossom in time,
Nurtured by faith in a rhythm sublime.

As the rain falls softly, our spirits are fed,
In moments of stillness, we honor the thread.
Threads of forgiveness, stitched in the heart,
Beneath grace's canopy, we never part.

With hands open wide, we gather the light,
Sharing our blessings, embracing the night.
In unity's comfort, our voices blend true,
Beneath grace's shelter, love's promise imbues.

Together we wander through shadows and glow,
In the arms of devotion, our faith will grow.
Beneath the vast heavens, we sing our refrain,
In the dance of our spirits, love shall remain.

Boundless Love in Offerings of Faith

In every gesture and action we share,
Love is the vessel, lifting us rare.
With open hearts we gather to give,
In the warmth of belonging, we truly live.

Each offering tender, a promise we make,
To cherish our neighbors, for love's own sake.
Through trials and triumphs, we journey as one,
In the light of His grace, our battles are won.

The tapestry woven, with threads pure and bright,
Shows boundless devotion through the darkest night.
In the folds of our faith, compassion becomes,
A beacon of hope to all hearts that are numb.

With gratefulness flowing, our spirits ignite,
Fueling the love that will banish the night.
In offerings shared, our purpose we find,
United in faith, transcending the blind.

Together we reach for the heights of His love,
A tapestry grounded in grace from above.
Boundless in measure, our hearts learn to soar,
In offerings sacred, we open the door.

Threads of Devotion in the Heart

In the chambers of faith, our devotion takes flight,
Stitched with the love that can banish the night.
With each loving thread, we weave stories true,
A tapestry vibrant, reflecting the new.

Gathering moments, we cherish each day,
In humility's gaze, we learn to obey.
Through trials and joys, our spirits entwined,
In the web of our souls, we are never confined.

Every prayer lifted, a thread pulls us near,
Binding our hopes, dispelling our fear.
In the quiet of night, our intentions take shape,
Threads of devotion help us to escape.

With open arms, we embrace the divine,
In the fabric of life, His love will shine.
Through each thread we journey, hand in hand we tread,
In the heart of the faithful, where angels have led.

So let us be woven, each part plays a role,
In this grand design, we honor the whole.
Threads of devotion, together we stay,
In the warm light of faith, we flourish and sway.

The Pinnacle of Our Divine Connection

In silence, we gather, hearts aligned,
A whisper of grace in the sacred wind.
Together we rise, our spirits entwined,
Guided by love, where all journeys begin.

Through trials and joys, we find the way,
Each moment a blessing, a light that shines.
In faith's embrace, we choose to stay,
The pinnacle reached, where divinity binds.

With hands raised in prayer, we seek the dawn,
The beauty of life, in each gentle breath.
In the warmth of hope, our fears are withdrawn,
We bask in the light, transcending all death.

Connected by spirit, we dance in truth,
The rhythm of love, unbroken and pure.
In the garden of kindness, we nurture our youth,
Where every soul's purpose, we gently secure.

Embracing the now, in sacred embrace,
As the stars bear witness, our hearts ignite.
Through each fleeting moment, we cherish the space,
In the pinnacle of union, our souls take flight.

A Blessing Over All That We Are

In the morning's glow, let gratitude rise,
A blessing unfolds, wrapped in love's grace.
For every heartbeat, and every sigh,
We cherish the gift of this sacred space.

With open hearts, we share our dreams,
The tapestry woven, thread by thread.
Each life is a story, or so it seems,
In the light of each dawn, we're gently led.

Compassion flows freely, a river wide,
With kindness, we water the seeds of peace.
As we lean on each other, together we bide,
Embracing the love that will never cease.

Let laughter echo, let joy take flight,
In each whispered prayer, a promise remains.
For all that we are, we'll shine ever bright,
As blessings surround us, in love's gentle chains.

In the evening's hush, let us take a pause,
Reflect on the journey of love's sweet embrace.
In gratitude, we rest, for this is our cause,
A blessing over all, in life's sacred space.

The Vessel of Shared Spirit

Within this vessel, a spirit flows,
A harmony forged in the fires of trust.
With every heartbeat, our true essence shows,
Together we shine, as we know we must.

In the quiet, we seek the divine spark,
Through gardens of prayer, we lovingly roam.
The light in our souls ignites the dark,
As we gather the threads that lead us back home.

Each voice a note in a symphonic grace,
In unity's name, we rise and we sing.
Love's melody dances, time cannot erase,
For in every heartbeat, our spirits take wing.

Let the winds carry forth our humble plea,
As we navigate storms, together we'll stand.
With hope as our anchor, we sail the sea,
In this vessel of faith, we are hand in hand.

To honor our journey, and all that we share,
In moments of laughter and tears that we shed.
With gratitude deep, we find strength in prayer,
The vessel of spirit, where love's freely fed.

Interwoven Prayers in Time's Embrace

In the weave of the night, our prayers are sewn,
Threads of intention, shimmering bright.
Each sacred heartbeat, together we've grown,
In the fabric of time, we find the light.

With each whispered hope, the cosmos conspire,
To cradle our dreams in the arms of grace.
Embracing the warmth, we tend to the fire,
The glow of our love, a transcendent space.

In moments of stillness, we gather our might,
The echoes of prayer rise like stars in the sky.
Through trials of faith, we soar to great heights,
As interwoven spirits, we learn to fly.

Through seasons of change, our roots intertwine,
In shadows and light, we hold on to hope.
Each breath a reminder, the divine we find,
With love as our compass, together we cope.

As time stretches onward, may we always see,
The beauty in moments, forever we claim.
In the interwoven prayers, we are set free,
In unity and grace, we honor His name.

Milton Keynes UK
Ingram Content Group UK Ltd.
UKHW020043271124
451585UK00012B/1026

9 789916 898901